Greater Than a Tourist
Book Series
Reviews from Readers

I think the series is wonderful and beneficial for tourists to get information before visiting the city.

-Seckin Zumbul, Izmir Turkey

I am a world traveler who has read many trip guides but this one really made a difference for me. I would call it a heartfelt creation of a local guide expert instead of just a guide.

-Susy, Isla Holbox, Mexico

New to the area like me, this is a must have!

-Joe, Bloomington, USA

This is a good series that gets down to it when looking for things to do at your destination without having to read a novel for just a few ideas.

-Rachel, Monterey, USA

Good information to have to plan my trip to this destination.

-Pennie Farrell, Mexico

Great ideas for a port day.

-Mary Martin USA

Aptly titled, you won't just be a tourist after reading this book. You'll be greater than a tourist!

-Alan Warner, Grand Rapids, USA

Even though I only have three days to spend in San Miguel in an upcoming visit, I will use the author's suggestions to guide some of my time there. An easy read - with chapters named to guide me in directions I want to go.

 -Robert Catapano, USA

Great insights from a local perspective! Useful information and a very good value!

 -Sarah, USA

This series provides an in-depth experience through the eyes of a local. Reading these series will help you to travel the city in with confidence and it'll make your journey a unique one.

-Andrew Teoh, Ipoh, Malaysia

GREATER THAN A TOURIST- UTRECHT NETHERLANDS

50 Travel Tips from a Local

Annemarie van Veelen

The statements in this book are of the authors and may not be the views of CZYK Publishing or Greater Than a Tourist.

First Edition

Cover designed by: Ivana Stamenkovic

Cover Image: https://pixabay.com/photos/utrecht-netherlands-dom-tower-683516/

Image 1: By Pepijntje - Own work, CC BY-SA 3.0, https://commons.wikimedia.org/w/index.php?curid=4234990

Image 2: By Diliff - Own work, CC BY 2.5, https://commons.wikimedia.org/w/index.php?curid=1112993

Image 3: By Aat van den Heuvel, CC BY 3.0, https://commons.wikimedia.org/w/index.php?curid=56567006

Image 4: By Deelnemer8 - http://en.wikipedia.org/wiki/Image:Miffy_Statue_in_Utrecht.jpg, CC BY-SA 3.0, https://commons.wikimedia.org/w/index.php?curid=737836

CZYK Publishing Since 2011.

CZYKPublishing.com

Greater Than a Tourist

Lock Haven, PA

ISBN: 9798798990825

>TOURIST

50 TRAVEL TIPS FROM A LOCAL

BOOK DESCRIPTION

With travel tips and culture in our guidebooks written by a local, it is never too late to visit x. Most travel books tell you how to travel like a tourist. Although there is nothing wrong with that, as part of the 'Greater Than a Tourist' series, this book will give you candid travel tips from someone who has lived at your next travel destination. This guide book will not tell you exact addresses or store hours but instead gives you knowledge that you may not find in other smaller print travel books. Experience cultural, culinary delights, and attractions with the guidance of a Local. Slow down and get to know the people with this invaluable guide. By the time you finish this book, you will be eager and prepared to discover new activities at your next travel destination.

Inside this travel guide book you will find:

Visitor information from a Local
Tour ideas and inspiration
Valuable guidebook information

Greater Than a Tourist- A Travel Guidebook with 50 Travel Tips from a Local. Slow down, stay in one place, and get to know the people and culture. By the time you finish this book, you will be eager and prepared to travel to your next destination.

OUR STORY

Traveling is a passion of the Greater than a Tourist book series creator. Lisa studied abroad in college, and for their honeymoon Lisa and her husband toured Europe. During her travels to Malta, an older man tried to give her some advice based on his own experience living on the island since he was a young boy. She was not sure if she should talk to the stranger but was interested in his advice. When traveling to some places she was wary to talk to locals because she was afraid that they weren't being genuine. Through her travels, Lisa learned how much locals had to share with tourists. Lisa created the Greater Than a Tourist book series to help connect people with locals. A topic that locals are very passionate about sharing.

TABLE OF CONTENTS

Travel Bucket List
NOTES

DEDICATION

To all those who are trying to find their way in a new city, who may feel helpless when lost, who will come across the unexpected, and who will create memorable experiences along the way.

ABOUT THE AUTHOR

Annemarie van Veelen is native Dutch, born in a
town about two hours from Utrecht. Despite the
distance, she decided to study at Utrecht University.
During the many hours spent traveling by train, she
read a lot of books, and obtained a master's degree in
Literary Science. Fortunately, she explored more than
just books in her time as a student. She got to know
the city of Utrecht extremely well. Besides reading
books, Annemarie likes hiking, cycling and catching
up with friends over coffee or beer.

One thing she loved about Utrecht, is that it's one
of the most beautiful cities of the Netherlands.
Utrecht has typical Dutch houses and pretty canals,
just like Amsterdam, but without the crowds. Even
though Utrecht extends into a large urban area, it feels
like a big village. Furthermore, this city is less rainy
than other places in this country. The view of the
Dom Tower on a bright day is magical.

After her studies, Annemarie wanted to see the
world. She traveled extensively in Asia and Africa.
She lived in other cities, including Amsterdam. But
there's something about Utrecht that even Amsterdam

can't offer. It's like a cute historical village, but with all the amenities that you would expect from a city. When Annemarie had to move back to Utrecht for work, it felt like coming home. Even though she has known her way around the city for fifteen years, she never stopped exploring. This is one of the great things about Utrecht. When you've never been here before, it's fairly easy to find your way, but even after you get very well acquainted with all parts of the city, there will always be hidden gems that you didn't expect.

Picture: Annemarie van Veelen, close-up

HOW TO USE THIS BOOK

The *Greater Than a Tourist* book series was written by someone who has lived in an area for over three months. The goal of this book is to help travelers either dream or experience different locations by providing opinions from a local. The author has made suggestions based on their own experiences. Please check before traveling to the area in case the suggested places are unavailable.

Travel Advisories: As a first step in planning any trip abroad, check the Travel Advisories for your intended destination.
https://travel.state.gov/content/travel/en/traveladvisories/traveladvisories.html

Picture: Annemarie van Veelen during a hike

FROM THE PUBLISHER

Traveling can be one of the most important parts of a person's life. The anticipation and memories that you have are some of the best. As a publisher of the Greater Than a Tourist, as well as the popular *50 Things to Know* book series, we strive to help you learn about new places, spark your imagination, and inspire you. Wherever you are and whatever you do I wish you safe, fun, and inspiring travel.

Lisa Rusczyk Ed. D.
CZYK Publishing

WELCOME TO
> TOURIST

Panorama

View of the Oudegracht from the Dom Tower

Dom in Utrecht

Miffy statue at the Nijntjepleintje in Utrecht

INTRODUCTION

*"I haven't been everywhere, but
it's on my list"*

– Susan Sontag

There are so many wonderful places to discover in Utrecht. If you're only visiting for a couple of days, you will have to make some tough choices. Are you taking a walk around the star-shaped city center, or relaxing on a terrace with a view over the canals? Kayaking or exploring the Miffy Museum? Giant teapot or UFO? Lunch next to a windmill, or diner inside an old church? Getting the ice cream that everyone is talking about, or tasting 'Broodje Mario'?

Whatever you decide to do, any visitor in Utrecht ends up spending time admiring Dom Church. This gothic cathedral is the tallest building of the city, it's crazy to think about how it got split in two parts (I'll explain how that happened later). I lost count of the number of times that I bumped into a stranger, because we were both staring at the tower of the cathedral, high in the sky.

I'm not sure what I like best about Utrecht. It has this old world charm, the city center consists of beautiful canals and cute bridges. There is always something to explore. Utrecht seems to have an endless amount of hidden gardens, quirky shops and sun-drenched terraces. The city is big enough for people to be open-minded, yet small enough for people to be warm and welcoming. It feels like a big village. If you're visiting Utrecht, I'm very excited about the great times that you're going to have here!

Utrecht
Netherlands

Utrecht Netherlands Climate

	High	Low
January	42	32
February	44	32
March	50	35
April	57	39
May	64	46
June	69	51
July	73	55
August	72	54
September	66	49
October	58	44
November	49	38
December	43	34

GreaterThanaTourist.com

Temperatures are in Fahrenheit degrees.
Source: NOAA

Picture: Oudegracht

WELCOME TO UTRECHT

1. OVERVIEW OF THE CITY

'Utrecht' actually means two things: the province and the capital of the province, usually it's the latter. The province capital has a clearly defined city center. This center, east of the central train station, is where most shops are. When you look at a map, you can see that the inner city is shaped vaguely like a star. This is because Utrecht used to be a fortified city. The former fortifications make for a really nice hike, especially around Manenburg and the Sonnenborgh Museum.

Utrecht is a popular city, sprawling out in every possible direction. Tuinwijk, Wittevrouwen and further northeast are lovely urban areas with pleasant parks. The east mostly contains urban areas too. Way out to the east, there is the Uithof, the university center. Even though Utrecht University owns many beautiful old, stately-looking buildings in the inner city, most classes take place at the modern Uithof.

Southwest is Kanaleneiland, an area that is known for criminality and cheap housing. Here, you will also find neighborhoods that have a distinct charm, like Lombok and Oog in Al.

By contrast, Leidsche Rijn was built only recently, to accommodate more people. This soulless part of the city consists of houses that are mostly the same. Many people opt to live in the charming villages surrounding Utrecht instead. Housing in the city center is extremely expensive.

The Amsterdamsestraatweg is a road that starts in the inner city and leads all the way to Zuilen, a village out west. This road has phone shops, kebab restaurants and erotic shops. A bit shady, yet very lively street.

Northwest is Overvecht, one of the poorest areas in the city with the highest crime rates. If you're a tourist, this is a place to avoid. If you're staying for a longer period of time, and you start to know your way around, Overvecht offers opportunities for cheap housing.

2. GET A BICYCLE

The inner city center of Utrecht is fairly safe at night, though you may encounter some interesting people. A phrase often heard at night used to be: "Hey, do you want to buy a bicycle?" Homeless people used to sell stolen bicycles for rock-bottom prices. However, in the past decade the police have taken action to prevent this. However, at second-hand shops you can still buy cheap bicycles, the prices are a bit higher, the chances of the bicycles being stolen are much lower. A good second-hand bicycle shop is Achterop, next to the Jacobikerk (a pretty church).

There are excellent ways to use a bicycle without buying one. If you have an OV-chipkaart, a card that makes it easier to use public transport in the Netherlands, then you can cheaply rent bicycles (called 'OV fiets'), available at larger train stations. You pay per day. Or, you can rent a bicycle for a day against slightly higher prices, from private companies like Black Bikes.

I wouldn't recommend renting an e-bike, because Dutch cyclists can be aggressive, especially in Utrecht. On the main cycling roads, you'll be

19

surrounded by dozens of people trying to make their way from home to work or elsewhere, and you'll be in their way.

Wondering whether you really need a bicycle? It depends on your plans. Utrecht's city center is often praised for its compactness, so if you're only staying for a short while, you can explore the city by foot or bus. But in case you're staying for more than a week, or if your accommodation is in the outer reaches of the city, I recommend a bicycle.

3. APPS THAT WILL MAKE YOUR LIFE EASIER

If you're already acquainted with the most-used apps of the Netherlands, skip this section. But if you're new to the Netherlands, these are apps that will help you integrate into Dutch life more.

The first thing that people in the Netherlands do before planning anything, is checking the weather. Unfortunately, our country isn't known for warm weather. Even though Utrecht receives much more sunshine than other Dutch cities, it's always a good idea to check what the day will be like. To get an overview of the whole country, visit the KNMI website (Dutch weather institute). For a more detailed look of the amount of rain in the next three or eight hours, check Buienradar. To compare which days are best in the next ten days, I find that Weather.com usually gets most of it right. Keep in mind that this is the Netherlands, nothing is guaranteed in terms of weather, there's always the possibility of rain and harsh winds.

Now, how do you find your way from one place to another? For traveling between two larger cities by train, the website of NS (Dutch railways) is best, but if your journey requires other forms of transport, like buses or trams, check 9292.

For booking hotels and hostels, the usual apps apply. The majority of accommodation options in the Netherlands are on Booking.com (their app allows payment by credit card). In summer, it's smart to book ahead, before everything is fully booked, but in other seasons it often works to show up without a reservation.

When you go out with people, it's normal to split the bill, sometimes to the last penny. Tikkie is an app that lets you send a payment request without knowing somebody's bank account number.

If you want to order things online, please be aware that the Netherlands has its own platform. While many other countries rely on Amazon, we use Bol.com. How it works is very similar to Amazon. Unfortunately, the English version of Bol.com doesn't function quite so well yet, so my advice is to use the Dutch version (with Google Translate).

4. DRESS CODE

Weather apps are great for planning activities on sunny days, but in the end, there is a good chance that you'll encounter bad weather too. Most Dutchies opt for layering up, or at least bringing a jacket and a vest. Another thing to bring when the weather is cloudy or uncertain, is a foldable umbrella.

In general, Dutch people dress more casual. Compared to other countries, Dutch girls wear less make-up, and they choose flat shoes rather than heels. They love to wear jeans, even in summer you will see many people wearing jeans. Though in spring, there is a day when all girls simultaneously decide that it's time to wear skirts. This day is called 'rokjesdag' (skirt day) and heralds the arrival of quality spring weather.

Utrecht has many students, and many people that have an alternative lifestyle, so it's an interesting place for watching people.

In summer, the Dutch flock to the parks, so bring a picnic cloth. Utrecht has a few great parks.

To get through winter, get yourself some quality gloves and a beanie.

Compared to Dutch cities more close to the coast, like Amsterdam and The Hague, Utrecht is further inland. Due to the small difference in location, the coastal cities receive more rain, Utrecht's climate is more pleasant. This makes Utrecht a great place to stay!

5. WHERE TO STAY

One of the most affordable accommodation options is Stayokay. What makes it stand out is its location. In the middle of the city, you can look out over Neude, a busy square. There are people shopping, having drinks at the many cafés, and visiting the central library. If you need a supermarket or restaurant, it's literally a one-minute walk from here. Stayokay offers a choice between very basic dorm rooms and single/double rooms with private bathrooms. The private rooms are comfortable, small and low-priced.

For cheap stays that last longer than a month, try searching a room through the website of Kamernet.

If you're just looking for something close to central station for a couple of days, there are plenty of nice options, like the NH hotel.

If you've got more cash to burn, consider staying at Hotel Mitland. All rooms come with access to the spa, the fitness room and the private indoor swimming pool. This hotel is at its best when it's not too cold outside, as the outdoor terrace looks out over the water of the Voorveldse Polder, a cute park. If you're not staying at the hotel, but you want to enjoy the view, consider eating at the adjoining restaurant, Vlonders. The restaurant isn't cheap, but there are some affordable options on the menu.

Picture: Neude Square

SO MUCH TO SEE

6. THE MOST INSTAGRAMMABLE PLACES OF UTRECHT

Utrecht is a picturesque city, with many places to take great photos, though it's hard to find a spot where you can take the perfect photo. The attics near central station look cute, like the Zakkendragerssteeg.

The area around the canals, most notably the Oudegracht, is very pretty. Great places for taking pictures are bridges like Bezembrug and Gaardbrug. Another option is to take the stairs leading down the canals.

Of course, the most prominent feature of Utrecht is Dom Church, though it's prone to restorations that block it from the public view. When it's not being restored, don't take pictures too close, as they won't do justice to the grandness of this gothic church. Instead, take pictures that include one of the streets leading to Dom Church, like Zadelstraat. When it is in restoration, an alternative is taking pictures in the

Dom garden, as that's also a beautiful showcase of gothic architecture. Or, climb Dom Tower, to get a view of Utrecht's skyline.

7. ALL ABOUT DOM CHURCH

Whenever you get lost in Utrecht, a good strategy is to look if you can see the Dom tower. Dom Church (in Dutch: Domkerk, sometimes referred to as St. Martin's Cathedral) dominates the landscape of Utrecht's inner city. Built from 1254, it's a gothic church, with lots of intricate details. One thing I like to do when I have time to kill is just wandering around the church, admiring all the details. Take a close look at the pinnacles for instance, it must have been a major undertaking to build this church in that time.

One of the things that people are quick to notice, is that the church is separated in two parts. The tower is separated from the choir and transept. This happened during a heavy storm in 1674, causing the nave to collapse. Nowadays, there is a square where the nave used to be.

A fun fact about the tower is that it's the highest church tower of the Netherlands. Also, it's the tallest building in Utrecht. Looking for an original way to exercise? Consider climbing the tower. There are 495 steps to take! Please be aware that the church charges an admission fee to climb the tower.

What's left of the rest of the church, is definitely worth a look as well. With gothic architecture on the outside and stained-glass windows on the inside, there's always something to see. Dom Church never ceases to amaze me, no matter how many times I've been there. On bright summer days it looks radiant with light, on cloudy days it looks dark and gloomy.

Something you shouldn't miss out on, is the church garden. Officially, it's called Pandhof van de Domkerk. Although only very small, it's a serene oasis in the middle of the city. The garden is popular for people to get married, as the combination of greenery and gothic arches makes for pretty pictures.

Dom Church has more to offer if you're willing to go underneath the earth. To experience the so-called 'DOMunder', take the stairs and see what's beneath the square. These grounds have been converted into an underground museum, showing the remains of the ancient Roman fort that was situated in Utrecht. Parts of the walls are still intact. DOMunder also shows how Dom Church was developed throughout the Middle Ages, and what the storm was like that destroyed part of it. Bring warm clothes, as it's cold to go beneath the earth.

Picture: The garden of Dom Church.
Source: Pixabay

8. ROMAN RUINS

DOMunder isn't the only glimpse of what Utrecht was like in the time of the Roman Empire. There are more places where you can see the Roman foundations, dating back to around 50 AD. When you're getting a drink or food at one of the restaurants at the Vismarkt or around Domplein, pay attention when you go to the bathroom, as some establishments in this location have parts of the ancient Roman fortifications in their cellars. I always think it's fascinating that something that old isn't regarded as a monument or anything special, instead it's just part of the city as it is today.

To see more archeological remains of the Romans, visit Central Museum. Keep in mind though that this museum shows bits and pieces of other eras too. If you're not into museums, you'd better spend your time elsewhere. There's so much more to see!

9. WATCH LIFE GO BY AT WEERDSLUIS

The canals are what makes Utrecht so pretty. Not only in the city center, but also further out. If you head northwest, you will find the Weerdsluis. This is a small lock that can be opened for boats to pass through. When closed, it's possible to walk over the lock.

There's been a lock in this place for a long time, dating back to the seventeenth century. In the nineteenth century it was renewed. The lock is situated in a very pretty part of Utrecht, with quaint Dutch houses, each in their own size and style.

Probably, you won't find the Weerdsluis in many guidebooks, as it's just a small lock. But I want to share it with you, because this is a favorite place for Dutchies to hang out, especially in summer. They bring food and drinks, and just sit on the stairs, overlooking the water. Sometimes, there are small private boats or kayaks to watch. An excellent place to relax and enjoy the view.

Once you get bored at the Weerdsluis, Miffy's Square is right around the corner.

10. MIFFY IS EVERYWHERE

Close to Weerdsluis is a square dedicated to Miffy, the cartoon character. To use a rabbit as the main character of children's books, was an invention from Dick Bruna, an artist that lived in Utrecht. In Dutch, the character is called 'Nijntje', but as this is difficult to pronounce by speakers of most other languages, internationally the name 'Miffy' is used. Miffy is world-famous. Utrecht pays respect to Miffy in many places, like the unassuming square close to Weerdsluis, which has a statue of Miffy. The square is called Nijntje Pleintje (try pronouncing this).

Another homage to Miffy is the museum dedicated to this character. It's a playful museum, with fun activities for kids. Also, there's a shop and a café.

Furthermore, the municipality of Utrecht incorporated Miffy details in various places throughout the city. Right in front of the Bijenkorf (expensive warehouse), take a look at Miffy's Traffic Light.

Compared to other children's books, Miffy is drawn in a very clean, no-frills style. The intention of the artist was to create a blank space, so that kids develop their own fantasies. And Miffy is not the only artistic creation that Utrecht is famous for.

11. IS THAT A TEAPOT ON TOP OF A ROOF?

In 2013, an artist put a giant teapot on a roof. To make it easier to spot, it was moved a couple of times to a different roof, which was quite an undertaking. Hopefully at its permanent location now, it's regarded as one of Utrecht's icons.

The artwork is called the Celestial Teapot, a symbol for the everyday lives of people. I think that it fits well in a city like Utrecht. Also, the artwork is a reference to Russell's teapot. This is a concept from the philosopher Bertrand Russell. He argued that if there was a teapot that is too small to be seen, it would be up to the person that says the teapot exists to give proof, rather than for people that cannot see it to prove that it doesn't exist. The artist behind Utrecht's teapot gave this philosophical idea a playful twist, by putting a giant teapot on a roof.

For a while, I didn't know where to find the teapot. The central train station was being rebuilt for years, amidst the chaos the teapot was hard to spot. Now, the central train station and adjoining mall are more or less finished, making the teapot easier to find. When you look up, you will find that Utrecht has several art objects on top of buildings, the giant teapot is only one of them.

Picture: Artwork at Central Station

12. IS THAT A UFO?

One of the artworks that are iconic for Utrecht's skyline, is the UFO, situated on top of the Inktpot building, close to central station. The best place to take a photo is south, from a small distance.

The building was built starting in 1918. The owner of the building is Prorail, a government organization responsible for the maintenance of the Dutch railway system. The building is called the Inktpot (the inkwell), it's one of Utrecht's most famous buildings.

What I love about the Inktpot is its austere look. Walking around the building, you can see that even its doors and other architectural details match with its style. Inside the building, a large colony of bats resides.

If you're interested to learn more about the Dutch railways, consider visiting the Spoorwegmuseum. This railway museum has its own railway station, a train will take you there from Utrecht CS in seventeen minutes. The museum contains an old signal box, the oldest steam locomotive of the country, and many miniatures. Also, the museum shows how Jews were transported to concentration camps in WWII. It's chilling to take a look inside one of the transport cars that were used during the war. If this is not for you, Utrecht has other museums that are worth checking out.

13. UTRECHT'S MOST FAMOUS HOUSE

On the outskirts of the city, you will find the Rietveld Schröder House. This house was built in 1924 by architect Gerrit Rietveld for Mrs. Truus Schröder-Schräder. Mind you, her first name is a typically Dutch name, her last name isn't. The artist, Gerrit Rietveld, was one of the most prominent artists of De Stijl, an art movement that Piet Mondrian was part of too. Their style is very abstract, based on simplified shapes.

The movement is known for the colors it used: only black, white and primary colors. Unfortunately, on the outside, the Rietveld Schröder House is mostly white and gray. Nonetheless, with its oddly shaped architecture, it's a popular place for people to take selfies.

Honestly, I would recommend taking a peek from outside rather than buying a ticket to see the inside of the house. Online it's possible to download a free map of the Rietveld Route, to see other houses that Rietveld designed too. However, it involves quite a distance, and other parts of Utrecht are more interesting for walking/cycling.

SPORTS

14. THE PERFECT WALK

The best way to see Utrecht's canals is a walk around the Grachtengebied, the area centered around the Oudegracht. This area is known for its 'werven', the wharves that line the water, below street level. Most wharves are adjoined by cellars that were used to store goods, hauled from ships. These wharf cellars date back to the early Middle Ages, though most have been converted to restaurants now.

A small walk takes you from central station to Dom Church, passing Winkel van Sinkel. To extend your walk a bit, go to Park Lepelenburg via Paushuize. Fun fact: Paushuize is where the only Dutch pope ever to exist has lived. From here, either get back to the station via Janskerkhof and Neude, or continue on a longer walk. From Park Lepelenburg, follow the former fortifications of the city (shaped like a star on the map), pass the Sonnenborgh Museum, finish at Manenborgh. Then there are two ways to get back to the city center, both are beautiful. Either continue along the green Rijnkade or follow the Oudegracht, on the other side of the canal from Eetcafé de Poort (which, by the way, is a nice place for a break).

Picture: Canals in Utrecht. Source: Pixabay

15. KAYAKING

Utrecht makes for pleasant walks, but there might be an even better way to see the city. Go to a rental shop, have your pick, and get onto the water. Enjoy the view!

There are various kinds of kayaks and boats to rent. I recommend choosing a kayak, as that offers the most flexible way to get through the canals. In summer, the canals are busy with tour boats. Kayaks are small. Often they come with bags to keep your valuables dry (or else, leave them in your hotel). There are kayaks that fit two people, but you will see plenty of couples that opt for solo kayaks. Safety comes first.

If you have small kids, consider renting a paddle boat. This is easier to fit in small children, it's slower and there's less risk of tilting the balance.

Whether you choose a kayak or paddle boat, Utrecht is beautiful from the water. The prettiest places include Drift and Kromme Nieuwegracht. Both the inner city and outskirts of Utrecht are interesting to explore.

16. HIKING AT LANDGOED RHIJNAUWEN

If you're willing to go further east of the city, visit Landgoed Rhijnauwen, between Utrecht and Bunnik. This estate comprises both forests and open fields. Here, you will walk through stately-looking lanes, beautiful any time of the year.

An intriguing monument of the estate is Rhijnauwen Castle, built in the eighteenth century. The estate itself dates back even further, estimates say the thirteenth century. If you look closely at the castle, you might be able to spot the remains of what it used to look like.

In the nineteenth century, a fort was built, called Fort Rhijnauwen. The fortifications are well-preserved, and they're among the largest in its kind. In WWII, the Germans used the fort to store munition and to execute members of the Dutch resistance. For a long time after the war, the fort was still being used to store munitions.

Online you will find a map of the estate. A highlight is Theehuis Rhijnauwen. This cute tea house offers delicious food, most people come for pancakes. When the temperatures aren't too bad, the outdoor terrace is popular. A great place to treat yourself after a hike!

TIME TO RELAX

17. THE CITY BEACH

Most Dutch cities have a city beach, even inland, but they're not as nice as coastal beaches. In Utrecht, a popular city beach is located in Oog in Al. This oddly named neighborhood is mostly urban, but at the tip, looking out over the water of the Amsterdam Rijnkanaal, is the beach.

There's a restaurant that serves food and drinks, named SOIA, an abbreviation for Strand Oog in Al. The menu has plenty to choose from, for kids too. Either enjoy your drink at a table in the sand, or bring it with you to relax in the grass. Either way, this place has a pleasant view, over the canals and a yellow bridge. What's fun about the Amsterdam Rijnkanaal is that it's quite busy with boats. Some modern, some very old. The city beach is open in winter and in summer, though it's much more popular in summer. Don't worry, Utrecht has plenty more places to relax!

18. THE BEST PLACE FOR WATCHING PEOPLE

Other than the city beach, there are several hotspots that people visit in the summer. One of these hotspots is Roost aan de Singel. This is a small restaurant, surrounded by a large swath of grass. People use this as a spot for picnicking. Some people get food at the restaurant, some bring their own. The restaurant food is okay, but it's nothing special.

What draws people here is the location, right at a bend of the Singel. In summer, the river is like a parade of people trying to find their way on the water, in kayaks, sups and small boats. Unfortunately, in winter there's nothing to see and the restaurant closes. When it's a bit cold, other places are better for watching people, like parks.

19. WHICH IS THE BEST PARK?

Utrecht's parks are popular for running, walking and enjoying the sun. Although of course it's possible to visit whichever park is most close to where you are, some parks in Utrecht are dull, others are delightful.

Most people like Wilhelminapark best. On a warm summer day, this is the place to be. It has lakes, fountains, and plenty of space for people to hang around on picnic cloths. Also, it has a promenade, so it's great for a short walk.

If you're at Wilhelminapark, consider making a detour to Rosarium. This is a small rose garden, dating back to 1911, lined by ornate white gates. I love how delicate the gates look.

My personal favorite is Julianapark. Although it's a bit out of the way, if you happen to be near Amsterdamsestraatweg, the park makes for a nice place to relax. What I like about Julianapark, is that there's both open space and tiny, hidden paths that hardly anyone takes. Other parks, like Griftpark, are not so impressive. If it's too cold outside to hang around in parks, consider visiting a sauna.

20. RELAX IN ONE OF THE BEST SAUNAS OF THE NETHERLANDS

Whether you just want to chill or whether you want to escape the bad weather, there are multiple saunas in and around Utrecht to choose from. By far the best is Spa Sereen.

One of the reasons that Spa Sereen is one of the best wellness resorts of the country, is that it's quite big, there are so many places to relax. Situated by a lake, most lounge chairs come with lake views. Also, the saunas are very good, and the resort offers five star service.

To visit Spa Sereen, my advice is to make a reservation. Please be aware that this is a full nudity sauna, there are no ladies-only days, everybody is welcome. If you have a large towel, a bathrobe and flip-flops, then bring them, to save money on having to rent these items. Technically, Spa Sereen isn't located in Utrecht but in Maarssen, a wealthy village just outside of Utrecht. It's a hassle to get there by bus, and taking a taxi is expensive. But trust me, it's worth the effort.

21. FEEL LIKE YOU'RE PART OF THE ELITE

Another place where Utrecht's elite gather to relax is the Louis Hartlooper Complex. This place is more than just a cinema. It features art house movies, often introduced or explained by speakers that are very educated about the subject. Before you go see a movie, always check the language. Most movies are in English with Dutch subtitles, but the Louis Hartlooper Complex airs many foreign language movies too.

The Louis Hartlooper Complex is especially popular among university students and teachers. Did you know that Utrecht University consistently ranks among the 100 best universities of the world? The university is part of what makes Utrecht a very pleasant place to be. Throughout the day, students and their professors gather in faculties, scattered around the city. At night, the intellectual elite gathers at the Louis Hartlooper Complex, including many alumni. One thing that I like to do is have a drink at the restaurant that's part of the complex. It offers lunch and dinner too. An excellent place to unwind, meet interesting people, and watch movies that you've never heard of. A true indulgence!

LET'S GO SHOPPING

22. SHOP 'TILL YOU DROP AT HOOG CATHARIJNE

There have always been shops right next to the central train station, but only in recent years this mall has become what it is today. Upon exiting the station at the northeast, you will first reach a large square before entering the mall itself. The square is lined by restaurants, a convenient place to eat, viewing over the square. The roof over the square, consisting of gray circles, has become one of the hallmarks of Utrecht.

Inside the mall, you will find all major chain stores, like Douglas, Primark, H&M etc. In comparison to other Dutch malls, Hoog Catharijne is quite large, and it's multi-storied. Also, it looks luxurious, with plenty of space for decorations like fountains and water works. The idea behind Hoog Catharijne is that it should be more than just a traditional retail center, it's intended as a place where people enjoy spending time. Also, the owners try to attract people with higher incomes. It's still being developed, but it's already very popular (and crowded). If you're more into small boutiques than chain stores, it's better to look elsewhere.

Picture: Hoog Catharijne

23. VINTAGE STREET

The Voorstraat is an interesting street, for multiple reasons. This is where you will find most vintage shops in the city. Unfortunately, as the quality of the vintage items is quite high, the prices are high as well. Still, it's a good street to hunt for unique clothing.

One of the shops in the Voorstraat is Sussies Vintage. This shop has clothes, shoes, handbags and other accessories (depending on current supply). Most clothes are for women, some for men. Here, you will have a good chance of finding unique 70s or other vintage clothing.

Apart from vintage shops, the Voorstraat has several coffee shops (not the kind where you drink coffee). This has to do with the street's history. A side street, the Hardebollenstraat, used to be a hotspot for window prostitution. The prostitutes have been banned from this street for years now, and the area has replaced much of its former shady character by gentrification and nice vintage shops.

24. A GIFT FOR YOUR LOVED ONES (OR YOURSELF!)

Utrecht has various gift shops and other outlets that sell touristy stuff. A fairly big store, with some original items, is KECK & Lisa. They sell home decorations, bags, stuffed animals, toys, greeting cards, etc. Also, they have a number of items that are shaped like Dom Church, or that otherwise remind you of Utrecht.

The store itself is a bit small, but it's filled to the brim with stuff. Things can be a bit expensive, but you will find some items here that you won't find in other shops. If you want to buy things that you can also find in other shops, then compare prices with Groeten uit Utrecht, a gift shop in the same street (Zadelstraat). Groeten uit Utrecht is smaller, but some items might sell cheaper here. Close to the gift stores, you will find other shops that sell curious items.

25. CONNECT WITH YOUR INNER NERD

One of Utrecht's most famous shops is Blunder, which sells comic books. I know what you're thinking, if you never read comic books, why would you go here? I'm not into comic books, but I still love checking out this store. With over 12,500 titles, it's amazing to browse through all the things they sell here. Often when I'm browsing, I realize that I know more about comic book heroes than I would have thought.

Blunder sells all the big names, but some unknown stuff too. They have X-Men, Batman, Sandman, The Avengers, and many more. Other than that, they offer an assortment of manga.

If you want even more nerdy things, then head to the other side of the canal, to Subcultures. This shop sells board games. Every board game that you know of, plus many that you probably never heard of, are being sold here. The owner is very friendly.

Board games and comic books aren't for everyone, though. If you're the type of person that's rather outside enjoying the sun than indoors playing board games, don't worry, Utrecht has got you covered.

26. EVERYTHING YOU NEED FOR ADVENTURE

If you need more outdoor clothes, or you forgot to bring some travel items, Utrecht is a great city for buying outdoor stuff. There are several well-stocked outdoor stores to choose from.

First, Kathmandu is legendary. This store has all the big brands that you would expect from a travel store. The prices are high, but the quality is too. Kathmandu has a large assortment of winter jackets.

Another shop worth checking out is JoHo. They sell everything you might need to travel, or to get inspiration for your next trip. Guidebooks, maps, backpacks, gadgets, etc. They sell original gifts too. Another plus is that JoHo is run by friendly people.

If you want to buy the best outdoor brands for the lowest price, make sure to check out the Bever outlet store too, conveniently located in the same street as JoHo. The Bever outlet sells leftover items, with large reductions. You need to be lucky to find something here that you're looking for, but if you do, it does save money.

Still can't find what you're looking for? Utrecht also has Decathlon, located in, you guessed it, the same street as JoHo & Bever outlet. At Decathlon you will find cheaply produced items at rock-bottom prices. They're very convenient if you need things like camping gear, runner's shoes, or cycling gear. Also, if you underestimated Dutch weather, and you're in need of an extra rain jacket, this is a good place to search.

EAT LIKE A LOCAL

27. IN THE BASEMENT

't Oude Pothuys is a restaurant that is situated in a basement. Everybody loves it. A staircase leads you down below, where you can enjoy dinner. The basement is beautifully lit, with lighting that creates a cozy atmosphere. Keep in mind that the basement has a low ceiling, choose your seat wisely if you're a tall person.

The food at 't Oude Pothuys is simple and affordable. On some days, they serve cheese fondue. I like to linger after having dinner, because it's also just a great place to enjoy a beer. 't Oude Pothuys regularly hosts live musical performances. You've probably never heard of the artists and bands, as this is more of a restaurant than a music venue, but the music creates a bond among visitors. When the sun is out, 't Oude Pothuys puts up a terrace that overlooks the canals.

28. EAT IN A WHARF CELLAR

One of the must-do's in Utrecht, is to eat at the wharves down by the canals. In summer, most wharf restaurants have a terrace with beautiful views over the water. In other seasons, you're better off sitting inside, much warmer and cozier.

There are several good restaurant options at the wharves. My personal favorite is Il Pozzo, a good Italian restaurant. Their pizzas are delicious. They serve all the classics, like margherita, salami, tonno and quattro formaggi. The pizzas are very affordable, meat and fish dishes are more expensive. Their salads are nice too, at reasonable prices. But Il Pozzo is famous for their pizzas. Fun fact: this was the first restaurant in Utrecht to choose its location in a wharf cellar. The Italian that came up with this idea, also invented Broodje Mario, a sandwich that Utrecht is famous for.

Picture: Terrace of Il Pozzo.
Source: Pixabay

29. UTRECHT'S MOST FAMOUS FOOD

Among the quintessential experiences that Utrecht has to offer, you should of course visit Dom Church, the wharf cellars, Hoog Catharijne etc. But another thing that the city is famous for is Broodje Mario. This isn't a fancy restaurant, it's just a hole-in-the-wall that sells sandwiches.

So why is it famous? In 1977, an Italian entrepreneur started selling sandwiches at the Oudegracht. He put cheese, salami, chorizo and peppers. To make sure that the sandwiches weren't too spicy for the Dutch, he used only very mild peppers. Broodje Mario became a big success. Nowadays, his shop still serves sandwiches at the Oudegracht, both the original recipe and all kinds of variations. The dough is made fresh every day. Broodje Mario also serves slices of pizza, but it's famous for its sandwiches. Honestly, they're not that special, but if you find yourself getting hungry in the afternoon, this is the spot for a cheap and tasty sandwich.

30. THE LIVELIEST TAPAS BAR OF UTRECHT

Okay, you're in the Netherlands, and if you're curious to sample authentic Dutch cuisine, then a tapas bar is not what you're looking for. But, if I'm being honest, Dutch cuisine just isn't that great. There is a good chance that you'll end up eating all other kinds of food from all over the world when you're in the Netherlands.

Tapas bar El Mundo has nice food, a central location and a great ambiance (it feels like you're in Spain). When you're looking for a place nearby in the center of Utrecht, this is one of the best quality restaurants to choose from. El Mundo is a stone's throw from central Neude square.

You can order the tapas dish by dish, or get a plate of mixed tapas, or get unlimited tapas. Either way, keep in mind that this is not the kind of restaurant you visit when you have only limited time available. I once spent four hours here (that was including cocktails, but you catch my drift). Take your time. El Mundo's outside terrace is okay, but the best tables are the ones upstairs, by the windows.

Most dishes at El Mundo are fish or meat centered, but it's possible to go all vegetarian too. For vegans, the options are minimal. Luckily, there are excellent vegan restaurants nearby!

31. BIOLOGICAL VEGAN FOOD

When I'm in the city center with vegan friends, Gys is the place that we go to. This restaurant offers 100% biological food. All dishes can be ordered gluten-free. The dishes are either vegetarian or vegan. While other restaurants offer only a few vegan options, Gys has plenty.

Of course, they have vegan hamburgers and fries. They also serve curries, noodles and more original vegan meals. Personally, I really enjoy their desserts. They serve various cakes. It's amazing how tasty vegan cakes can be! Another plus of this restaurant is that the prices are very agreeable.

32. IF YOU HAVE A BIT MORE TO SPEND

The prices at the Watertoren are high, but they come with a view. The restaurant is located inside an old water tower, at the two upper floors. From here, you can see the canal of the Vaartsche Rijn, and part of Utrecht.

Please be aware that the tower is quite far from the city center. Built between 1906 and 1907, the intricate details show that the tower was part of Renaissance Revival Architecture. If you have time, walk to the other side of the river to take better photos of the tower.

The menu consists of four or five courses. There's a vegetarian version too. Each dish is beautiful in how it looks and tastes, you can tell that much thought went into each dish. Keep in mind that on special occasions, like Christmas and New Year's, this venue will be fully booked.

33. FANCY HIGH TEA?

There are plenty of savory food options in Utrecht, but sometimes you want something sweet. Then, the best place to go is the Bakkerswinkel, conveniently located near the city center. When you walk in, the first thing you see is the bakery. Here, they sell bread, cakes and other delicacies. It's a cute shop. There have been bakeries in this location since the eighteenth century.

Downstairs is the restaurant where they serve cake, lunch and, in the winter months, cheese fondue. A local favorite is high tea. The Bakkerswinkel is fabulous at making all kinds of sweet pastries that most people have no idea how to make. Curds, brownies, savory pies, etc. The high teas are also available gluten-free, lactose-free, or vegan. The restaurant's ambiance is very cozy, a nice place to spend time.

If you don't feel like having a high tea, then I recommend getting scones, which taste fantastic because they're freshly made. The scones with clotted cream and homemade jam are the best that the Bakkerswinkel has to offer. And if you have a sweet tooth, there's more to discover in Utrecht.

34. LET'S GO TO ROBERTO

When people in Utrecht say they're visiting Roberto, it means they're going to get ice cream. This Italian ice cream shop won multiple prizes, one of them being the world champion in making ice cream. If you're not convinced yet, go get a taste yourself!

Roberta Gelato offers both traditional and creative flavors. There's vanilla, strawberry, stracciatella, chocolate, pistachio, hazelnut, lemon, etc. But they will also have flavors that you've never heard of, like frollini. Some flavors are available with sugar substitutes or rice milk.

The shop is located in the Poortstraat, a bit out of the way from the city center. This area has many historical buildings, though, making for a pleasant walk. Please be aware you will not be the only person in Utrecht longing for Roberto's creations. The chances of getting a table in summer are very slim, as Roberto Gelato is only a small hole-in-the-wall. On sunny days, the queue for takeout often extends outside the shop. Trust me, the ice cream is worth the wait.

Don't feel like going all the way to Roberto's? In summer, there's an ice cream cart at the Jansbrug, right in the center of the city. It's called Venezia. Don't expect it to be as good as Roberto's, but still, it's fairly tasty.

DRINK LIKE A LOCAL

35. CENTRAL SQUARE

One of the most popular places to have a drink is Neude. This central square is surrounded by bars and cafés. An excellent spot to have a drink, whether it's a coffee on the outside terraces in summer, or a beer cozy inside during winter. The cafés and bars are all more or less the same, just have your pick and find a table.

When you're at Neude, please do check out the old post office. This is the stately looking building at the west side of the square. Built starting in 1919, it was used as Utrecht's central post office for decades. Now, it's used as a library and a center for cultural events. If you don't dare to go inside, at least have a peek inside the doors that open up to the square. Just behind the doors you will see a black figure saying "Europe", an artwork that is part of the monumental building.

One of the things that I like about Neude is that there's so much to see. Each house around the square is painted in a different color, making for a nice picture. If you enjoy hanging out in places that come with a view, there's more to discover in Utrecht.

36. VISIT A WINDMILL

A comfortable place to relax during daytime is Molen De Ster. This windmill dates back to 1739, it was rebuilt between 1996 and 1998. Originally, there were dozens of windmills in and around Utrecht, of which twelve were used to saw wood. Of these, only two remain, Molen De Ster is one of them. It offers a rare opportunity to see a windmill up close in a big city like Utrecht.

The café of the windmill is a popular place, especially on the weekends. The terrace looks out over the water (great for spotting ducks and geese). As there's a playground too, the windmill attracts families with kids. Sometimes there are concerts, art exhibitions and other cultural events. The small farm has chickens and pigs. The café serves coffee, smoothies, beer, and wine, as well as a simple lunch. This kid-friendly place makes for a nice opportunity during daylight hours to see a windmill up close. In the evening, other places are more suitable for hanging out.

37. INSIDE A BEAUTIFUL OLD CHURCH

My personal favorite for food or drinks in Utrecht is Café Olivier. Located inside an old Catholic church, this place is very atmospheric. All tables and chairs are made from wood, and even though the building isn't used as a church anymore, it contains original decorations like maria statues and a pipe organ dating from 1890. This church makes you feel like you're surrounded by history.

The food at Café Olivier is fine. Mostly, it's traditional pub food. If you're in for a traditional Dutch snack to go with some alcoholic drinks, consider getting 'bitterballen'. These are small meatballs, deep-fried with a crunchy crust.

One of Café Olivier's features is that it's a Belgian beer café. Even though Dutch beer is appreciated worldwide (i.e. Heineken), the Dutch believe that

Belgian beers are better. Olivier is a great place for sampling Belgian beers. If you don't know which beers to choose, ask the waiter to surprise you.

38. MORE BELGIAN BEERS

To taste the weirdest of beers, visit Kafé België. This is a much smaller bar than Olivier, but it has over 200 beers to sample. Ever heard of beer that tastes like dessert? Or you want to get the best IPA there is? Kafé België is the place to be!

As said, it's a small place, often crowded on the weekends. There's a cat too. What I usually do is walk by and peek through the windows to see whether there's the right amount of people. If not, then I pick another place to go. Occasionally, Kafé België holds a pub quiz or a bingo, it may be required to register for these kinds of events. When there's a soccer game that involves Belgium, this is a good bar to watch the game. Please be aware that Kafé België is very no-frills, down-to-earth, and it doesn't serve food.

Picture: View over the Oudegracht

PARTIES & CONCERTS

39. WINKEL VAN SINKEL

Winkel van Sinkel is wonderful for several purposes. On a hot summer day, it has a terrace outside, perched on the corner of the canals, a great place to watch people go by. This terrace is very sunny in summer, good for tanning.

Besides drinks, Winkel van Sinkel also serves food. Winkel van Sinkel is located in an old monumental building, both its exterior and interior are beautiful. Another plus is that it's huge, so there are always plenty of seats. The restaurant is a bit posh, but the food is nice. As Winkel van Sinkel has its own sommelier, the wines are matched with the menus. A fun activity is to try a couple of wines with a "wine arrangement" (basically, a mini wine tasting).

At night, the place turns into a party place, at least on Friday and Saturday. Then the music is turned up and the monumental hall gets colored by the disco lights. Occasionally, there are concerts or other cultural events.

The name "Winkel van Sinkel" was derived from the merchant Anton Sinkel. He sold fabrics, first in Amsterdam, later on in Utrecht. Winkel van Sinkel became famous in Utrecht, even though it's not used as a fabric warehouse anymore. The name has become synonymous with a store that sells a bit of everything and anything.

Now, Winkel van Sinkel isn't a warehouse anymore, instead it's a pleasant place to enjoy some drinks or food. The downside is that it's a bit posh, so usually it's not the liveliest of places. To party like crazy, you better go elsewhere.

40. THERE'S ALWAYS SOMETHING HAPPENING AT TIVOLI

Tivoli is a concert venue with two locations: one right next to the central train station (Tivoli Vredenburg) and one far away from the city center (Tivoli De Helling). The central location has more events, and they manage to book more well-known artists and bands. The far-away location has alternative parties and ditto music. Each location has its own website, listing the bands that are playing.

Tivoli Vredenburg is a huge modern building, with six concert halls and many spaces in between. Classical concerts mostly take place in the Grote Zaal and Hertz, big seated halls that are centered around a symphonic stage. Large club nights are in Ronda and Pandora. Jazz, slightly alternative music and all small concerts are in Club Nine and Cloud Nine, on the top floor. If you're visiting a concert that happens to be taking place on the top floor, that means you're going a long way up by escalators and stairs. Look out for Park 6, this is an upper-floor square that is used as a rooftop bar in summer. Also, it hosts yoga sessions.

Downstairs in Tivoli Vredenburg is a bar named Het Gegeven Paard, convenient for having a drink before a concert (or for just hanging out, without visiting a concert). When the weather isn't too bad, the outdoor terrace spills out onto the banks of the Singel. The name of the bar is derived from a Dutch saying "je moet een gegeven paard niet in de bek kijken". This means you shouldn't check the teeth of a horse that was given to you (a method to measure the horse's age). When something is given to you, you should be grateful and not ask too many questions. This is an old Dutch saying.

At the other side of town, you will find Tivoli De Helling. This is a place that you only go to when a band of your liking happens to play here. It hosts artists in several genres, like rock, metal, indie, ambient etc.

41. ALTERNATIVE MUSIC

If you enjoy alternative music styles, then another place to check out, besides Tivoli De Helling, is ACU. This former squatters' home hosts concerts and club nights. At the front of the building, there's a bar, a nice place to get a drink and meet interesting people.

On some days, they serve a vegan three-course dinner for an extremely low price. The goal here is to reduce food waste. If I'm being honest, the dinners here aren't my favorite, but ACU is great for seeing alternative bands perform. They prefer cash, so hit the

ATM before you visit. The bar is run by volunteers, make sure to be nice to them.

The building used to be owned by Auto Centrale Utrecht, a car company. Decades ago, the building was taken by squatters. ACU was renamed Anarchistisch Centrum Utrecht. Throughout the years, the squat scene in the Netherlands faced more stringent legislation and law enforcement. ACU became more of a cultural/political center and concert hall than just a home for squatters. In the end, it managed to keep its iconic location, aided by the municipality of Utrecht.

Is ACU too alternative for your liking? Not a worry, because just around the corner, you will find a completely different venue.

42. PARTY LIKE A STUDENT

For students, the most popular discotheque in Utrecht is Woolloomooloo. Run by student association Utrechtsch Studenten Corps (USC), it's only accessible if you have a student identity card.

Woolloomooloo has quite a bit of history. When the Netherlands were taken by the Germans in WWII, the Germans used the building of the student association as their headquarters in Utrecht. After the war was over, people found out that the Germans had built a bunker behind the building. From 1970, this bunker has been used as a discotheque. Since then, a lot of drugs and alcohol have been consumed here.

43. HAVE SHOTS AT CHUPITOS

Chupitos is the shot bar of Utrecht. Like Woolloomooloo, you need to show a student identity card to get in here. Right around the corner from Neude, it has a central location. A good last place to visit on a party night!

At Chupitos, they serve hundreds of different kinds of, you guessed it, shots. Some are very colorful, some are on fire, some have foam. The idea of Chupitos is that having shots can be an experience in itself. Whatever you make of it, Chupitos is a fun place to try a couple of creative shots.

44. FOLLOW THE LIGHTS

Whether you're with friends or alone, a nice way to spend the evening is by viewing Trajectum Lumen. This is a form of art that incorporates light; multiple artists collaborated to project various hues of light on Utrecht's city center. The walk takes about one-and-a-half hours, you can find a route map of Trajectum Lumen online. Though it's possible to book a private tour guide, it's cheaper to follow the route by yourself, it's fairly easy. The light is projected starting from the moment the streetlights are turned on in the evening. The light show ends at midnight. You can see it every day of the year.

If you don't have time to walk the entire route (or if it's too cold), I find that the most beautiful part of the route is Tunnel Ganzenmarkt. This tunnel is lit in green, pink, purple and yellow.

45. LGBTQ+ IN UTRECHT

Just like Amsterdam, Utrecht has its own canal parade. Utrecht Canal Pride is held annually in June.

A very popular event, it draws visitors from all genders and sexual orientations.

A hotspot for queer people at any time of the year is Savannah Bay. This book store specializes in topics relating to gender studies and being queer. Savannah Bay has a bar that houses lectures, discussion nights and book signings.

Also, Utrecht is home of the most famous LGBTQ party of the Netherlands, PANN. You may wonder, why is this the most famous one in the country? Why not one of Amsterdam's many gay hotspots? The answer is that PANN welcomes young people from whatever orientation, so it attracts many gay people, but it's also very friendly to straight people. The obstacles to visiting a party like PANN are often lower for people than going to COC (local LGBTQ+ organization).

PANN is a massive party, but it's nothing compared to Utrecht Canal Pride. The city becomes very crowded during the Pride, because many inhabitants of Utrecht come to see it and show their support (gay and straight alike). However, there is one event in Utrecht that draws an even bigger crowd.

46. CELEBRATING KING'S NIGHT & KING'S DAY IN UTRECHT

Being in Utrecht around King's Day is a treat! Celebrated annually by the end of April, it's a Dutch party where all people wear orange clothes to celebrate the King's birthday. Traditionally, the cities turn into giant outdoor flea markets where people can sell their old stuff. You will see everything here: clothes, barbies, furniture, old records, street food etc.

Arguably, Utrecht is a better city to celebrate King's Day than Amsterdam. On this day, the capital is even more overflowing with tourists than it is on a normal day. I find it too crowded. In some places in Amsterdam, it's difficult to even get to the next street, because it's that crowded. Utrecht receives fewer visitors, still it's very lively. Some places in Utrecht get crowded too, notably the area around the Drift. In Amsterdam, it's difficult to find the best place to be, because the flea markets and parties are scattered around the city. In Utrecht, it's much easier to find the best place to be, as the city center is more compact.

Something you shouldn't miss out on, is King's Night. This is celebrated on the evening of the day before King's Day. Utrecht is famous for hosting the best King's Night of the country. This evening, everybody is outside in their orange clothes, selling their belongings on the streets. This evening is known for drinking and consuming street food.

DAY TRIPS FROM UTRECHT

47. CYCLING ALONG THE VECHT

A favorite pastime of many inhabitants of Utrecht is to cycle along the Vecht. This river flows all the way from Utrecht to Ijsselmeer, but you don't need to go that far to see the prettiest parts. There are several shops where you can rent a bicycle or e-bike, for instance at central station.

The Vecht starts at Weerdsluis, close to the city center. After a while, you will reach Slot Zuylen, a castle surrounded by lush gardens. Buy a ticket to enter both the castle and its gardens, or get a ticket for the gardens only.

After another stretch of this bendy river, you will see Oudaen and Nijenrode Castle. The latter is used as a secluded, upscale university.

In case you still have the energy to keep going, then visit Loenen aan de Vecht. This is often named as the most beautiful village in the province of Utrecht. With cute houses and a couple of restaurants, it's a good place to stop for coffee or food. From Loenen aan de Vecht, it's possible to cycle back to Utrecht via the Loosdrechtse Plassen, but personally, I find it better to just cycle back along the Vecht. It's easier, prettier, and in certain times of the year there are lots of flies around the Loosdrechtse Plassen. If you get tired of cycling, go to the nearest train station (Breukelen), remember to buy a ticket for yourself as well as your bicycle.

Wherever you go exactly, the area around the Vecht river is well suited for cycling. This part of the country is quite flat, dominated by farmland. If you'd rather visit hilly forests than flat farmlands, then head east instead of west of Utrecht.

48. EXPLORING UTRECHTSE HEUVELRUG

This hilly area is excellent both for hiking and for cycling. Don't set your expectations too high, there aren't any high mountains, just some very gently sloping hills. Still, Utrechtse Heuvelrug has beautiful forests. Intersecting the forests are straightforward paved cycling roads, as well as tiny footpaths.

On a bicycle, you can get to Utrechtse Heuvelrug by cycling north, past the Berenkuil. Though it takes quite a while before you reach the forest. A quicker way to start is to grab a train to Driebergen-Zeist and start from there. You can cycle as long or as short as you like.

Part of Utrechtse Heuvelrug, the Kaapse Bossen are beautiful, and they provide a good amount of elevation. You can get to Kaapse Bossen on a bicycle from one of the nearest train stations, Driebergen-

Zeist or Maarn. If you're not bringing a bicycle but hiking, then take a bus directly from Utrecht Central Station to Kaapse Bossen. It takes a long time, it's also possible to get off earlier, somewhere else in Utrechtse Heuvelrug, to start your hike. If you do reach Kaapse Bossen, enjoy the look over the surrounding landscape from Uitkijktoren De Kaap. You're better off skipping this watchtower if you're afraid of heights, though.

Another highlight is the Pyramid of Austerlitz. Yes, it's really a pyramid! Not quite the same as those in Egypt, though. Basically, it's an overgrown monument on top of a hill. It was erected in 1804 by soldiers of Napoleon. For some good exercise, take the stairs to the top of the pyramid. Please be aware that there's an entry fee to enter the premises. Also, look carefully at the distances involved. If you're renting a bicycle, consider whether you want an e-bike or a regular bicycle. Reaching the Pyramid of Austerlitz by public transport is difficult. However, when you manage to get there, it's a lovely area to explore.

49. A PRETTY LITTLE LAKE

Close to the Pyramid of Austerlitz lies Henschotermeer. This man-made lake is surrounded by inland dunes, meaning there's soft sand to lounge on. The lake is a great place for putting your feet up and tanning. In the middle of the lake is an island, reachable by two bridges.

Please be aware that Henschotermeer is privately owned, there's an entry fee. This puts some people off, though in summer it's a popular place nonetheless. I think Henschotermeer is an excellent opportunity to escape the busy streets of Utrecht. Here, you will be surrounded by forest instead.

In case you're more into culture rather than nature, the province of Utrecht has plenty to offer as well. How about visiting a beautiful castle?

50. THE LARGEST CASTLE OF THE NETHERLANDS

In a village close to Utrecht, you will find Castle De Haar. Built starting in 1892, it is part of Gothic Revival Architecture. Baron Etienne van Zuylen van Nijevelt (that's his complete name) inherited ruins, on which he decided to build the castle. The castle was meant to commemorate his rich family. In Paris, he met a woman that he married, Hélène de Rothschild. Together they decided that the castle should have all possible luxuries, to impress their wealthy friends. They had the village of Haarzuilens moved to the east, to open up space for creating a Roman garden. Despite it being the nineteenth century, they had running hot water, central heating and a Turkish steam bath. At a certain point, they possessed more luxuries than the queen of the Netherlands.

This castle is a joy to visit, because it provides a glimpse of the luxurious lives that the baron and baroness lived a century ago. Many paintings, antique chairs and gothic ornaments remained in place. To visit the castle, get a train to Vleuten, then get a bus to

Haarzuilens. From there, it's still quite a walk, but the village is lovely to see as well.

Inside the castle, there's a shop that sells souvenirs. Aside from things like keychains and mugs, they also sell honey that is produced in the garden of the castle. Another special product are silk shawls, uniquely designed for the castle.

Picture: Castle De Haar. Source: Pixabay

BONUS: SOUVENIRS TO BRING HOME

Most museums have their own shops, but in the city center of Utrecht you will find souvenir shops as well. Not the crazy amount that you will find in Amsterdam, though (and that's a good thing!). Besides Zadelstraat, another street to check for gift shops is Steenweg.

Something fun to bring home is an item with Dom Church printed on it. In Utrecht, you can get about anything that you can think of showing Dom Church: keychains, magnets, calendars, paintings, notebooks, greeting cards, mugs, puzzles, candles, etc.

If you like Miffy, consider getting a stuffed animal. Gift shops sell these in all colors. They make great gifts for kids too. Can't get enough of these? In Vinkenburgstraat, close to Neude, you will find Pinokkio Speelgoed. This toy store has many stuffed animals, both Miffy and other characters. They sell wooden toys too.

Other things to get at gift shops are items that show old Dutch houses, each in their own size and style, sometimes depicted on blue and white porcelain. For instance, you could get plates, mugs or bowls. Some items show bicycles, which are iconic for the Netherlands, particularly Utrecht. Another popular souvenir are wooden clogs, either tiny ones on a keychain, or stuffed clogs that you can use as slippers to keep your feet from getting cold.

BONUS: SOLO TRAVELER TIPS

Life as a solo traveler can be tough. You may feel lonesome among the crowds, you need to make every decision by yourself, and sometimes you just don't know what to do. As Dutch people tend to go out in small groups and stick to their groups, the Netherlands isn't the easiest place for making new friends. But, once you've made contact, people tend to be interested in talking, and almost everyone speaks English fairly well. There are numerous ways to meet people in Utrecht.

An excellent opportunity to approach people is when you're about to attend an event that you both like. This way, there's a good chance that you have something in common, like shared hobbies or taste in music. You could for instance check out which concerts are playing at Tivoli Vredenburg, pick one of your liking, and have drinks beforehand at Het Gegeven Paard (the bar downstairs of the concert halls). Another thing to check, is whether any events are happening, as the city of Utrecht traditionally hosts many festivals. In summer, Utrecht's parks serve as gathering places for all kinds of groups.

If you're staying at a hostel, that's a great place to meet people too. The Stayokay in Utrecht is very spacious, unfortunately not the best place to meet people. The Bunk Hotel has separate pods to sleep in, which doesn't make for an easy place to meet either. Strowis Hostel is very social and cozy, with lots of opportunities to meet interesting people, but it's not the cleanest of hostels. Each hostel has its pros and cons.

Another way to meet people is to connect online first. Even though Meetup.com isn't as big in the Netherlands as it is in certain other countries, still, it's a low-key way to meet people that you share hobbies or interests with. You could share a passion for a certain kind of music, sports, board games or arts. Also, they have meet-ups that are women-only. Another option is to visit networking events, to chat with like-minded people.

Above are some tips for having a chat with people when you're feeling lonesome. If, however, you're the kind of solo traveler that loves to spend time on their own, then by all means, go for it. Utrecht is a fabulous city to explore, whether on your own or with company.

BONUS: THE BEST PLACES FOR COWORKING

Whether you need to do some unexpected work while you're on holiday, or whether you live as a digital nomad, there's a chance that you'll need a place to work. Don't worry! Utrecht has got you covered, the city has excellent options for coworking and using flexible workplaces.

First, the most comfortable places to work are Coffeecompany and Het Gegeven Paard. Both are cafés, located in the city center. Coffeecompany is near Dom Church. This café serves magnificent coffee, but it gets crowded with students. Het Gegeven Paard is the café downstairs in the large Tivoli building. It's a nice bar, on the first floor you will find more space. Het Gegeven Paard stimulates people to work there, by rewarding frequent visitors with extra coffee.

Looking for more space? Then check out The 5th. This is a lunch bar located on the first floor of the Stayokay Hotel at Neude. It's spacious, much like a canteen, with views over the central Neude square.

Don't want to stray too far from the central train station? Or just need to get something done quickly, without a hassle? Get coffee or tea at Bar Beton, and plug in your laptop. This café is located on the first floor of the train station, just take the flights up near Starbucks. Admittedly, there's a Starbucks here, and also one at the corner opposite Miffy's Traffic Lights, but I personally find that these locations are too busy. With so many customers coming through, there are better options for working in Utrecht than Starbucks.

If you want to save money, there are some free options too. The Central Library, inside the old post office building at Neude, has multiple areas to work or study. Keep in mind that you need to be quiet here. Another option is the Uithof. If you're a student, you will find plenty of seats scattered in the Uithof's many buildings. Please be aware that the Uithof is far away from the city center, reachable by tram, it's intended only for students and their teachers.

So, what if you're looking for an inspiring place, but you don't want to work in cafés or student centers? A social way of coworking is booking a spot at Seats2Meet. The concept is that you're welcome to do your work here, as long as you're willing to share your knowledge with other professionals, in any conversations that might arise. This way, people can learn from and inspire each other. You need to register online to secure a spot. It's right next to the central station.

Wherever you decide to open your laptop, don't work for too long, because the city of Utrecht is out there waiting for you to discover. Try opening this book on a random page, or asking a random stranger for advice. There's always something to do. Happy exploring!

PACKING AND PLANNING TIPS

A Week before Leaving

- Arrange for someone to take care of pets and water plants.

- Email and Print important Documents.

- Get Visa and vaccines if needed.

- Check for travel warnings.

- Stop mail and newspaper.

- Notify Credit Card companies where you are going.

- Passports and photo identification is up to date.

- Pay bills.

- Copy important items and download travel Apps.

- Start collecting small bills for tips.

- Have post office hold mail while you are away.

- Check weather for the week.

- Car inspected, oil is changed, and tires have the correct pressure.

- Check airline luggage restrictions.

- Download Apps needed for your trip.

Right Before Leaving

- Contact bank and credit cards to tell them your location.

- Clean out refrigerator.

- Empty garbage cans.

- Lock windows.

- Make sure you have the proper identification with you.

- Bring cash for tips.

- Remember travel documents.

- Lock door behind you.

- Remember wallet.

- Unplug items in house and pack chargers.

- Change your thermostat settings.

- Charge electronics, and prepare camera memory cards.

READ OTHER
GREATER THAN A TOURIST
BOOKS

Greater Than a Tourist- California: 50 Travel Tips from Locals

Greater Than a Tourist- Salem Massachusetts USA50 Travel Tips from a Local by Danielle Lasher

Greater Than a Tourist United States: 50 Travel Tips from Locals

Greater Than a Tourist- St. Croix US Birgin Islands USA: 50 Travel Tips from a Local by Tracy Birdsall

Greater Than a Tourist- Montana: 50 Travel Tips from a Local by Laurie White

Children's Book: Charlie the Cavalier Travels the World by Lisa Rusczyk Ed. D.

> TOURIST

Follow us on Instagram for beautiful travel images:
http://Instagram.com/GreaterThanATourist

Follow *Greater Than a Tourist* on Amazon.

CZYKPublishing.com

> TOURIST

At *Greater Than a Tourist*, we love to share travel tips with you. How did we do? What guidance do you have for how we can give you better advice for your next trip? Please send your feedback to GreaterThanaTourist@gmail.com as we continue to improve the series. We appreciate your constructive feedback. Thank you.

METRIC CONVERSIONS

TEMPERATURE

110° F —   — 40° C
100° F —
90° F —   — 30° C
80° F —
70° F —   — 20° C
60° F —
50° F —   — 10° C
40° F —
32° F —   — 0° C
20° F —
10° F —   — -10° C
0° F —   — -18° C
-10° F —
-20° F —   — -30° C

To convert F to C:

Subtract 32, and then multiply by 5/9 or .5555.

To Convert C to F:

Multiply by 1.8 and then add 32.

32F = 0C

LIQUID VOLUME

To Convert:...............Multiply by
U.S. Gallons to Liters............... 3.8
U.S. Liters to Gallons 26
Imperial Gallons to U.S. Gallons 1.2
Imperial Gallons to Liters....... 4.55
Liters to Imperial Gallons 22
1 Liter = .26 U.S. Gallon
1 U.S. Gallon = 3.8 Liters

DISTANCE

To convert ....Multiply by
Inches to Centimeters 2.54
Centimeters to Inches 39
Feet to Meters...................... .3
Meters to Feet 3.28
Yards to Meters 91
Meters to Yards 1.09
Miles to Kilometers 1.61
Kilometers to Miles............ .62
1 Mile = 1.6 km
1 km = .62 Miles

WEIGHT

1 Ounce = .28 Grams
1 Pound = .4555 Kilograms
1 Gram = .04 Ounce
1 Kilogram = 2.2 Pounds

99

TRAVEL QUESTIONS

- Do you bring presents home to family or friends after a vacation?

- Do you get motion sick?

- Do you have a favorite billboard?

- Do you know what to do if there is a flat tire?

- Do you like a sun roof open?

- Do you like to eat in the car?

- Do you like to wear sun glasses in the car?

- Do you like toppings on your ice cream?

- Do you use public bathrooms?

- Did you bring a cell phone and does it have power?

- Do you have a form of identification with you?

- Have you ever been pulled over by a cop?

- Have you ever given money to a stranger on a road trip?

- Have you ever taken a road trip with animals?

- Have you ever gone on a vacation alone?

- Have you ever run out of gas?

- If you could move to any place in the world, where would it be?

- If you could travel anywhere in the world, where would you travel?

- If you could travel in any vehicle, which one would it be?

- If you had three things to wish for from a magic genie, what would they be?

- If you have a driver's license, how many times did it take you to pass the test?

- What are you the most afraid of on vacation?

- What do you want to get away from the most when you are on vacation?

- What foods smell bad to you?

- What item do you bring on ever trip with you away from home?

- What makes you sleepy?

- What song would you love to hear on the radio when you're cruising on the highway?

- What travel job would you want the least?

- What will you miss most while you are away from home?

- What is something you always wanted to try?

- What is the best road side attraction that you ever saw?

- What is the farthest distance you ever biked?

- What is the farthest distance you ever walked?

- What is the weirdest thing you needed to buy while on vacation?

- What is your favorite candy?

- What is your favorite color car?

- What is your favorite family vacation?

- What is your favorite food?

- What is your favorite gas station drink or food?

- What is your favorite license plate design?

- What is your favorite restaurant?

- What is your favorite smell?

- What is your favorite song?

- What is your favorite sound that nature makes?

- What is your favorite thing to bring home from a vacation?

- What is your favorite vacation with friends?

- What is your favorite way to relax?

- Where is the farthest place you ever traveled in a car?

- Where is the farthest place you ever went North, South, East and West?

- Where is your favorite place in the world?

- Who is your favorite singer?

- Who taught you how to drive?

- Who will you miss the most while you are away?

- Who if the first person you will contact when you get to your destination?

- Who brought you on your first vacation?

- Who likes to travel the most in your life?

- Would you rather be hot or cold?

- Would you rather drive above, below, or at the speed limited?

- Would you rather drive on a highway or a back road?

- Would you rather go on a train or a boat?

- Would you rather go to the beach or the woods?

TRAVEL BUCKET LIST

1.

2.

3.

4.

5.

6.

7.

8.

9.

10.

NOTES